2.52

T292977

Baby Foxes

Bobbie Kalman

🌱 Crabtree Publishing Company

www.crabtreebooks.com

It's fun to learn about Baby Animals

Created by Bobbie Kalman

Dedicated by Michael Golka
To Russell—keep your wits sharp and your humor cunning
Love, Dad

**Author and
Editor-in-Chief**
Bobbie Kalman

Editor
Kathy Middleton

Proofreader
Crystal Sikkens

Photo research
Bobbie Kalman

Design
Bobbie Kalman
Katherine Berti
Samantha Crabtree (cover)

Production coordinator
Katherine Berti

Photographs
BigStockPhoto: pages 4–5, 14, 15 (top left),
    21 (bottom right), 23 (top left)
Shutterstock: cover, pages 1, 3, 5 (right), 6 (top),
    7 (except bottom left), 8 (top), 9 (all bottom),
    10 (bottom), 11, 12, 13, 15 (bottom left),
    17 (bottom), 18, 19 (except top left), 20, 21
    (except bottom right), 22, 23 (except top left
    and middle left), 24 (except Arctic foxes,
    bat-eared foxes, dens, and kit foxes)
Other images by Corel, Creatas, Digital Stock,
    Digital Vision, Eyewire, and Photodisc

Library and Archives Canada Cataloguing in Publication

Kalman, Bobbie, 1947-
        Baby foxes / Bobbie Kalman.

(It's fun to learn about baby animals)
Includes index.
ISBN 978-0-7787-3960-9 (bound).--ISBN 978-0-7787-3979-1 (pbk.)

        1. Foxes--Infancy--Juvenile literature. I. Title.
II. Series: It's fun to learn about baby animals

QL737.C22K333 2010   j599.775'139   C2009-905194-X

Library of Congress Cataloging-in-Publication Data

Kalman, Bobbie.
  Baby foxes / Bobbie Kalman.
      p. cm. -- (It's fun to learn about baby animals)
  Includes index.
  ISBN 978-0-7787-3979-1 (pbk. : alk. paper) -- ISBN 978-0-7787-3960-9
(reinforced library binding : alk. paper)
  1. Foxes--Juvenile literature. 2. Foxes--Infancy--Juvenile literature. I. Title.
II. Series.

  QL737.C22K354 2010
  599.775'139--dc22

                                                      2009034818

Crabtree Publishing Company

www.crabtreebooks.com   1-800-387-7650

Printed in China/122009/CT20090915

Published in Canada
Crabtree Publishing
616 Welland Ave.
St. Catharines, Ontario
L2M 5V6

Published in the United States
Crabtree Publishing
350 Fifth Ave.
59th floor
New York, NY 10118

Published in the United Kingdom
Crabtree Publishing
Maritime House
Basin Road North, Hove
BN41 1WR

Published in Australia
Crabtree Publishing
386 Mt. Alexander Rd.
Ascot Vale (Melbourne)
VIC 3032

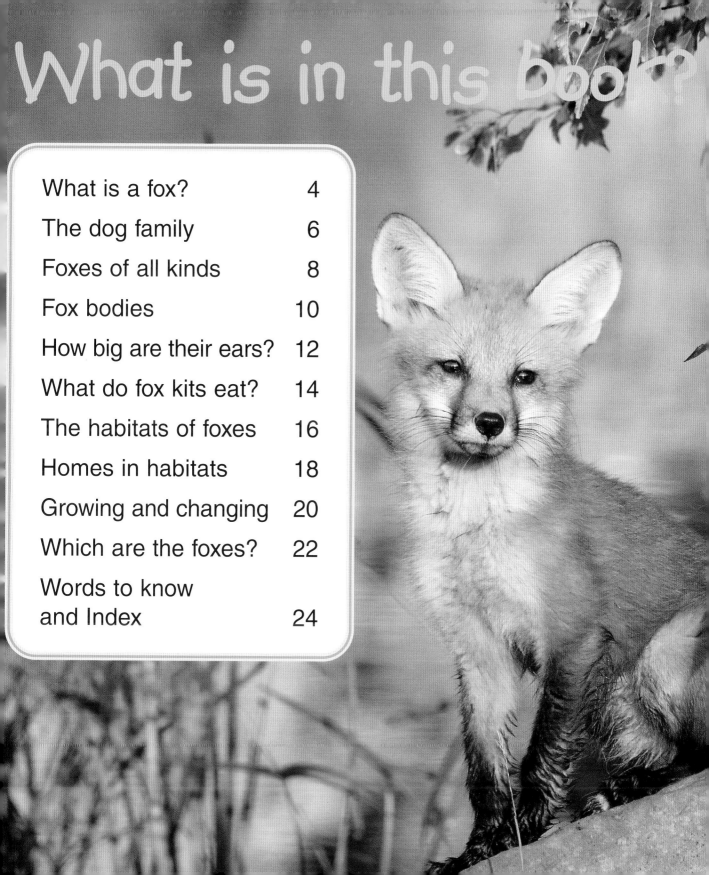

What is in this book?

What is a fox?

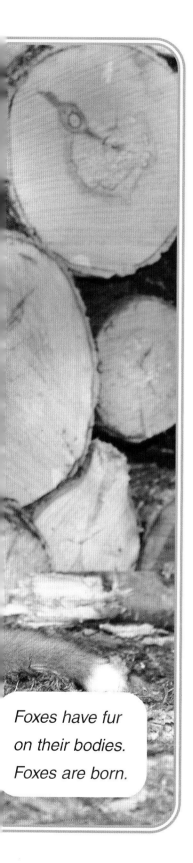

Foxes have fur on their bodies. Foxes are born.

A fox is an animal called a **mammal**. Mammals have hair or fur on their bodies. Mammals are **born**. They grow in the bodies of their mothers.

Drinking milk

Mammal mothers feed their babies milk. The milk comes from their bodies. Drinking mother's milk is called **nursing**. These baby foxes on the left are nursing. Baby foxes are called **kits**, **cubs**, or **pups**.

The dog family

Foxes belong to the *Canidae*, or dog, family. Foxes, wolves, coyotes, and jackals are **wild** dogs. Wild dogs live in nature. They do not live with people. **Pet** dogs live with people.

pet dog

Baby foxes are wild dogs. There are many kinds of foxes. These baby foxes are Arctic foxes. To learn about different foxes, turn to pages 8 and 9.

This spotted pup is an African wild dog.

This black-backed jackal is a wild dog.

This coyote pup is a wild dog.

Wolves are wild dogs, too.

7

Foxes of all kinds

red fox

There are more than 21 **species**, or types, of foxes. The red fox is the most common fox in the world. It lives almost everywhere. These pages show a few kinds of foxes. Foxes can be different colors and sizes.

Few foxes can climb trees, but gray foxes can! Each gray fox has a black stripe in the middle of its tail. The gray fox kits in this picture live in North America. The gray fox in the small picture lives in South America. It is a close relative of the North American gray fox.

The bat-eared fox uses its big ears to listen for and hunt insects. (See page 12.)

Arctic foxes are white in winter and gray in summer. Their fur changes color to help them blend in with their habitat. Blending in is called **camouflage**. Find out on page 13 why the ears of these foxes are so small.

Fennecs are the smallest foxes.

Corsac foxes live in Asia.

Cape foxes live in Africa.

Fox bodies

A fox has four legs, a bushy tail, and a pointed **muzzle**. Its body is covered in thick fur. The nose and mouth are part of the fox's muzzle.

Foxes have sharp teeth for eating meat.

Foxes have good senses of hearing and smell. They see well at night.

The fox uses its bushy tail to balance itself when it jumps.

Foxes have four toes with claws on each paw.

paw   claws

Red foxes have white fur on the underparts of their bodies.

Foxes are **vertebrates**. Vertebrates are animals with **backbones**. The bodies of foxes also have other bones. All the bones make up a **skeleton**.

backbone

fox skeleton

How big are their ears

Some fox ears are very big, some are small, and others are medium-sized. The ears of all foxes are pointed forward. Foxes are **predators**, or animals that hunt **prey**. Prey are the animals they hunt. By having ears that point forward, foxes can hear the sounds in front of them. It helps them find prey that is hiding.

Bat-eared foxes eat mainly insects. Their huge ears help them hear where insects are hiding under the ground. The ears also keep these foxes cool. Do you know why?

Warm-blooded animals

Foxes are mammals, and mammals are **warm-blooded** animals. Warm-blooded animals warm and cool their bodies from the inside. Animals lose heat through their ears. Big ears lose more heat. Small ears help keep heat inside the body.

Arctic foxes live in a freezing-cold place. Their small ears lose less heat and help keep their bodies warm.

Many red foxes live in places with both cold winters and hot summers. Their ears are medium-sized. They keep foxes warm in winter and cool in summer.

13

What do fox kits eat?

Most dogs are **carnivores**. Carnivores eat meat. Some foxes eat mainly meat. Arctic foxes hunt small animals such as mice and rabbits. They also eat the leftovers of dead animals that other predators have hunted. Bat-eared foxes eat insects. Some foxes, such as red foxes, are **omnivores**. Omnivores eat more than one kind of food. They eat meat, but they also eat plant foods such as fruit, leaves, seeds, and flowers.

After they are born, all fox kits drink milk. They also start eating other foods when they are about two months old. Red fox kits eat eggs, mice, fruit, and flowers.

This red fox kit has gone hunting with its mother. It has caught its first mouse.

These red fox kits are looking for food inside a dead log. Maybe they will find some ants or other insects to eat.

This fox kit has found an egg to eat.

When foxes cannot find meat, they eat plants.

The habitats of foxes

The natural places where animals live are called **habitats**. Foxes live in **forests**, **meadows**, **deserts**, and **tundras**. They also have homes in these habitats. Learn about their homes on pages 18 and 19.

Arctic foxes live on tundras. Tundras are cold, dry places. Trees do not grow on tundras.

Fox kits are baby foxes, but kit foxes are a kind of fox. These foxes are kit foxes. Kit foxes live in hot, dry deserts.

These red fox kits live in a meadow. A meadow is a field of grasses.

This red fox lives in a forest. Forests have many trees and other plants.

Homes in habitats

Some foxes dig their own **burrows**, or underground homes, in the habitats where they live. Other foxes find homes in dead logs or **caves**. Some move into burrows that were dug by other animals. The homes of foxes are called **dens**. The dens of baby animals are called **nursery dens**.

These fox kits live in a burrow. They are waiting for their mother to come home with food.

This kit lives inside a dead log.

This fox kit's den is a cave. A cave is a room inside a rocky hill.

This kit lives in a den under some rocks.

Growing and changing

fox kit

Foxes are born in **litters** of four to eight kits. Litters are two or more babies. The kits grow and change quickly. They are fully grown **adults** at ten months. Adult foxes can make their own babies. Each time a new baby is born, a new **life cycle** begins. A life cycle is the set of changes in an animal from the time it is a baby to the time it becomes an adult.

These one-month-old kits wait for their mother in their den. They still drink their mother's milk, but they will soon eat other foods, too.

As the kits grow, their mother takes them out of the nursery den to play.

The kits start hunting with their mother at twelve weeks.

*They learn how to **pounce**. To pounce is to leap on prey.*

The kits fight to find out who the strongest foxes are.

This mother fox has a litter of babies. Each baby starts a new life cycle.

Which are the foxes?

Foxes can look very different! Sometimes other members of the dog family also look like foxes, but they are not foxes. Test your fox skills and pick out the three pictures on the opposite page that contain foxes. Can you guess which animal or animals are coyotes, wolves, gray foxes, jackals, kit foxes, or cape foxes?

Answers:

1. wolves 2. kit foxes 3. jackal 4. cape fox
5. gray fox 6. coyote Numbers 2, 4, and 5 are foxes.

23

Words to Know and Index

Arctic foxes
pages 6, 9, 13, 14, 16

bat-eared foxes
pages 9, 12, 14

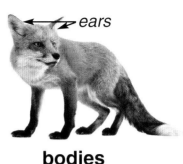

ears

bodies
pages 5, 10–11, 13

cape foxes
pages 9, 22

dens
pages 18–19, 20

food
pages 10, 12, 14–15, 18, 20

gray foxes
pages 8, 22

kit foxes
pages 16, 22

red foxes
pages 8, 10, 13, 14, 15, 17

backbone

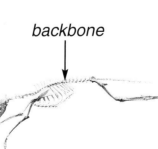

skeleton
page 11